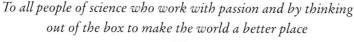

*To Sally, Mike, Jim, Nancy, and the many others working hard
in the fight against COVID-19*
—Suzanne

*To all people of science who work with passion and by thinking
out of the box to make the world a better place*
—Elisa

Special Thanks

My deepest gratitude to Dr. Joyce Almeida, June Almeida's daughter, for supporting this project by vetting the text and sketches, answering questions, providing primary sources, science papers, and photos, as well as intimate insights about her mother. The story of a person's life is much richer when it shares personal qualities and interests, along with facts and dates. This story includes many of Joyce's descriptions about her mother, such as curious, focused, creative, driven, social, intuitive, passionate about work, and voracious reader.

I also want to acknowledge these kind experts for their help:
Sally Hunsberger, PhD, and Michael Fay, PhD, NIH National Institute of Allergy and Infectious Diseases, Division of Clinical Research; Don Weaver, molecular biologist, NIH Immunology Lab; Erika L.F. Holzbaur, PhD, Professor, Perelman School of Medicine, University of Pennsylvania; Nichole Ladon and Lindsey McNeir, technicians extraordinaire.

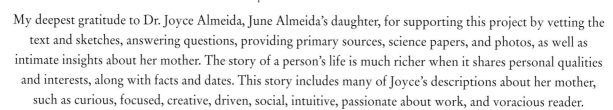

Library of Congress Cataloging-in-Publication Data
Names: Slade, Suzanne, author. | Paganelli, Elisa, 1985- illustrator.
Title: June Almeida, virus detective! : the woman who discovered the first human coronavirus / written by Suzanne Slade ; illustrated by Elisa Paganelli.
Description: Ann Arbor, Michigan : Sleeping Bear Press, [2021] | Audience: Ages 6-10 | Summary: "Scientist June Almeida's skill in using the electron microscope helped identify viruses, and when she was 34 years old, she discovered the first human coronavirus"— Provided by publisher.
Identifiers: LCCN 2020031508 | ISBN 9781534111325 (hardcover) Subjects: LCSH: Almeida, June D.—Health. | Scientists—Juvenile literature. | Scientists—England—London—Biography. Classification: LCC Q143.A46 S53 2021 | DDC 579.2092 [B]—dc23
LC record available at https://lccn.loc.gov/2020031508

JUNE ALMEIDA, VIRUS DETECTIVE!

The Woman Who Discovered the First Human Coronavirus

SUZANNE SLADE ✳ *Illustrated by* ELISA PAGANELLI

PUBLISHED BY SLEEPING BEAR PRESS™

JUNE'S FAVORITE DAYS WERE SCHOOL DAYS.
After the family breakfast, Dad headed out to work. Then June,
Mum, and baby Harry set off down the streets of Glasgow, Scotland.
They walked past Alexandra Park and the tenement buildings where
June's friends lived.

But when June saw her beautiful school, she ran as fast as her legs would go. She couldn't wait to get to class!

Always curious, June loved learning. Especially about her favorite subject —
science. She was excited to share her discoveries with her parents.
Little Harry listened, too (until something better came along!).

When June was ten, Harry became very sick. Soon, he passed away.
Sadness swallowed the family like a deep, dark hole.

Years flew by. June thought about Harry often, and treasured memories of him like priceless jewels.

As June grew, so did her passion for science. In biology, she discovered tiny cells make up the human body and learned how they each have jobs to do. June was so enthusiastic about science, she won the top science prize at school.

June was easy to talk to and had lots of friends.
After school, she read stacks of books.

Her favorites were science fiction.

Creative and observant, she loved photographing the
beauty (and surprises!) she found in nature. June was always
on the lookout for the perfect picture. She noticed small details,
and her keen eye helped her create stunning photos.

June dreamed of studying science at a university. But college was expensive. Her father was a bus driver, which didn't pay much. Her mother's job at a local shop didn't either. With no savings for college, she left school at age 16 to help pay the family bills.

June wanted to find a meaningful job. Fascinated by biology, she hoped to learn more about it. She also longed to help people with illnesses like her brother.

So she applied to work at the nearby hospital. With her top grades
and interest in biology, she was hired to work in the lab. She learned
to use a microscope to magnify and examine cells from sick people.
Her findings helped doctors treat patients.

In 1952, June's family moved to London, England.
She found a job in a hospital lab there.

On weekends, June strolled around London, admiring the sights.
One day she met an interesting artist named Henry.

They fell in love
and married.

The two decided to start their life together in Canada. With her experience, a new research lab in Toronto quickly hired her.

June began working with a
powerful electron microscope
that magnified things 25,000 times—
much more than microscopes
she'd used before!

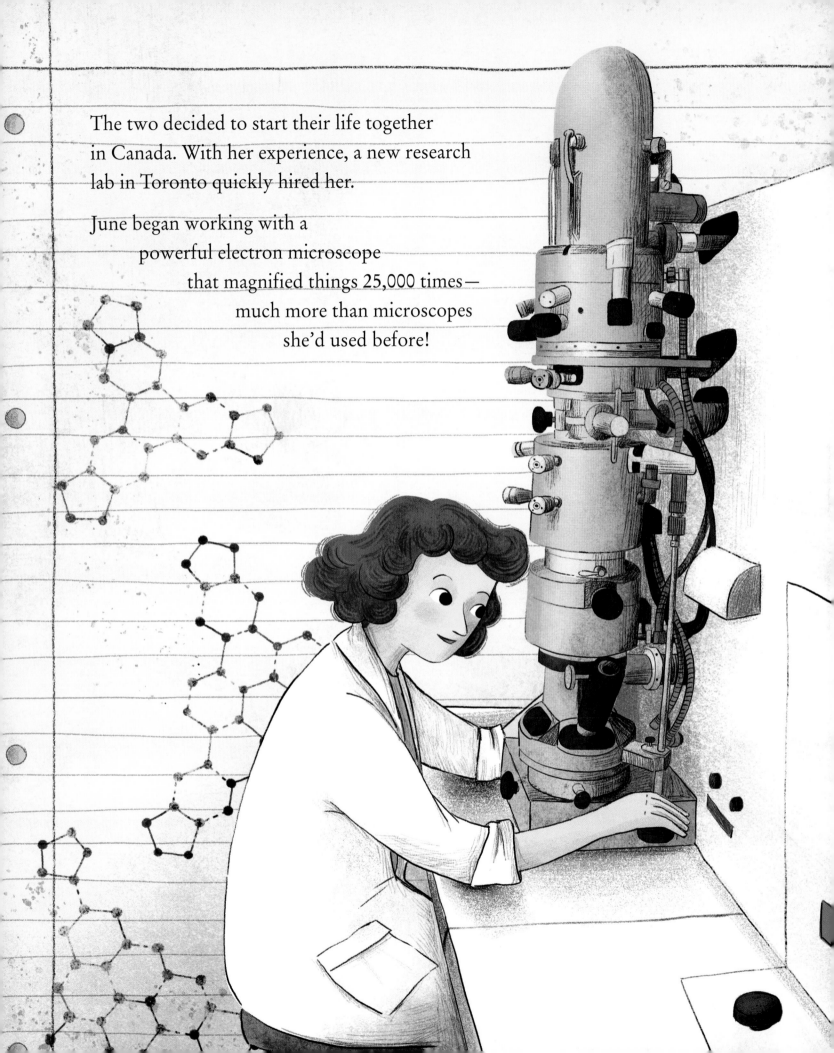

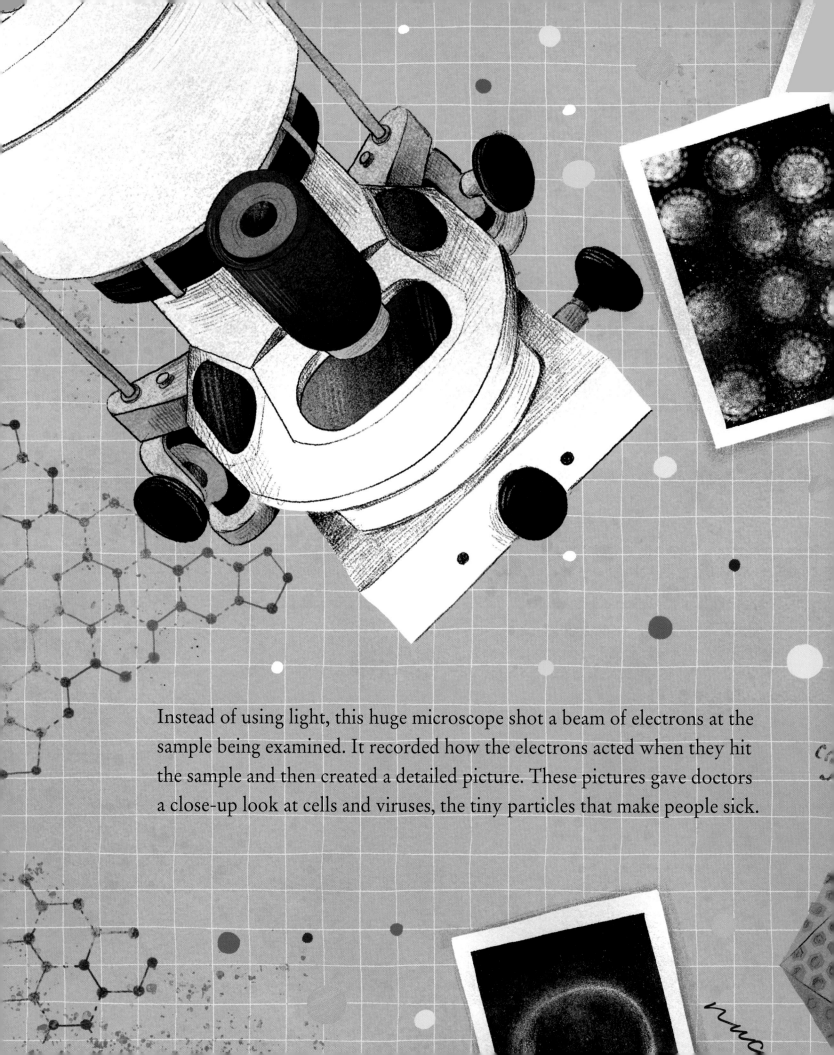

Instead of using light, this huge microscope shot a beam of electrons at the sample being examined. It recorded how the electrons acted when they hit the sample and then created a detailed picture. These pictures gave doctors a close-up look at cells and viruses, the tiny particles that make people sick.

The microscope's photos were helpful. But it was hard to tell which tiny blobs were viruses and which were cells.

A photographer at heart, June was determined to get better pictures. Then scientists could learn more about how viruses worked.

June pondered this perplexing problem.

She knew that when a virus made someone sick, their body created antibodies. Those antibodies would surround a virus, like tiny soldiers, to fight it. After destroying a virus, the antibodies remained to protect against future attacks.

June decided to see if antibodies would show her which blobs were viruses.

virus

antibodies

So she put antibodies and virus particles together. Using the electron microscope, she blasted them with an electron beam.

Like moths drawn to light on a dark summer night, the antibodies crowded around the virus—just as she'd hoped.

June's pictures astounded scientists! Her skill on the electron microscope created clear pictures that helped them find and study viruses

In 1960, June and Henry welcomed a new family member—a beautiful baby girl. June cherished her time at home with her daughter.

After returning to work, June continued her remarkable research, wrote science papers, and earned a promotion. She spoke to large groups eager to hear about her work.

A scientist at a London hospital was so impressed,
he asked June to join his lab. She was thrilled.
So her family packed their bags
and moved back to London.

Meanwhile, a researcher near London named David Tyrrell
was baffled by a virus that had given a young boy a nasty cold.
His entire team couldn't identify the mysterious virus.

Which made everyone wonder:
Was it a new virus?

David was skeptical anyone could
solve this mystery. But he'd heard June was
an expert at figuring out viruses that stumped
other scientists. So he asked her to help. She agreed,
and David shipped her the virus sample.

When it arrived, June couldn't wait to get started. Since it was an unknown virus, there were no antibodies to help find it.

But she knew a technique called negative staining that might work. After years of practice, she was quite skilled at it, too!

POTASSIUM HYDROXIDE

4%
Ph

First, June used a glass tool and water to separate the virus particles from the rest of the sample.

Then she added a drop of acid, which turned the liquid containing the virus particles black as ink. With this black background, the virus would be easier to see—like white chalk on a blackboard.

Using thirsty filter paper,
she removed the extra liquid.

Finally, June shot a beam of
electrons at the sample with her
microscope to create sharp pictures.

Then came the moment she'd been waiting for. Her well-trained eyes carefully scanned the picture.

She spotted the mystery virus!

Looking closely, she noticed each virus blob had tiny dots circling it like a crown.

June was stunned!

Years before she'd seen *two* other viruses that looked just like it—both from sick animals. In fact, she'd written a science paper about them. But researchers had rejected her paper because they didn't believe she'd found a new virus. They thought her pictures were just blurry photos of a common flu virus.

Now June had found a third virus
that looked like the other two.
It proved this *was* a new virus!

June met with doctors to discuss her incredible discovery. They thought the dots surrounding the virus looked like a crown, too. The Latin word for crown is *corona*. So they decided to name it coronavirus.

June and David published a paper with her pictures to tell others all about the coronavirus.

June greatly enjoyed her work. She also loved spending time with her husband and daughter. But Henry missed Canada and longed to move back. June couldn't imagine leaving her job or London.

Sadly, Henry returned to Canada and the two divorced.

Now a single mother, June was busier than ever.

Fueled by her passion, June kept studying viruses that made people sick, such as rubella, hepatitis B, and HIV.

She patiently created new virus images. Many appeared in medical books. Her pictures helped scientists develop medicines that could attach to viruses and block them from making people sick.

Years later, June retired from her research. But she still loved to learn.

She taught herself to play the flute, studied antiques, and fixed fine china.

She also learned how to use a digital camera. And, of course, she kept creating amazing pictures!

Poem by June Almeida
(With apologies to poet William Blake)

Virus, Virus, shining bright,
In the phosphotungstic night,
What immortal hand or eye,
Dare frame thy fivefold symmetry.

June Almeida modeled her humorous poem after William Blake's poem "The Tyger." The first two lines refer to the phosphotungstic acid she used to turn the liquid surrounding virus particles black, making it easier to see bright white virus particles. The last line describes a virus particle with five identical sections.

MORE ABOUT JUNE

June in Scotland, circa 1950

June around 1950, working in a lab at Glasgow Royal Infirmary

June Almeida was a dedicated virologist who spent decades studying viruses. A virus is a tiny particle that's too small for our eyes to see. There are about 10 nonillion (one with 30 zeros after it) different viruses on Earth. Fortunately, very few are harmful to people. June was extremely skilled at using an electron microscope to take detailed photos of virus particles. Her patience, persistence, and attention to detail were just some of the qualities she possessed that helped her create exceptional images.

June was only 34 years old when she discovered the first human coronavirus. Coronaviruses are actually a family of different viruses. Back then, scientists didn't think coronaviruses were a serious threat to people because they only seemed to cause common colds. While a cold is annoying, the human body can usually fight it off in several days.

Though June did not attend college, her research and science papers were so impressive that the University of London awarded her a master's degree in 1970. June's excellent work continued, and the next year she was awarded a doctor of science by the same university.

Through the years June made many discoveries, which she shared in more than 100 science papers she wrote or cowrote. In 1967, the paper she coauthored with David Tyrrell, "The Morphology of Three Previously Uncharacterized Human Respiratory Viruses that Grow in Organ Culture," informed scientists about the coronavirus. Her remarkable work also included creating the first image of the rubella virus, discovering that the hepatitis B virus is made of two components, and helping to publish high-quality images of the HIV virus, which causes AIDS.

In 2003, an illness called SARS broke out. It was caused by a coronavirus named SARS-CoV. Many people with the disease suffered from lung infections, which revealed how new types of coronavirus could be very dangerous to people. As researchers looked for answers to prevent and cure SARS, they turned to June's discoveries for help.

Today, scientists are studying a new coronavirus called SARS-CoV-2, which causes COVID-19. When this illness appeared in 2019, researchers used the technology and methods June developed to identify it as a coronavirus. June Almeida's groundbreaking work is providing scientists in the fight against COVID-19 with important tools and knowledge as they strive to create medicines and a vaccine to make the world a healthier place!

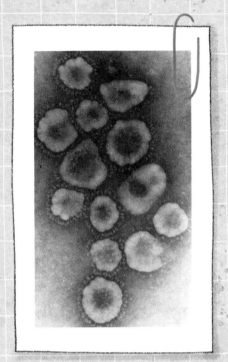

Image created by June of coronavirus particles

JUNE and the ELECTRON MICROSCOPE

June learned how to operate an electron microscope when she began working at the Ontario Cancer Institute in 1956. The type of microscope she used was a transmission electron microscope, or TEM. Instead of using a glass lens to focus light like ordinary optical microscopes, the powerful TEM shot a beam of electrons at the sample to be examined.

First, June put the sample she wanted to study on a tiny, round grid. Then she placed the grid in the TEM, which then sent a stream of electrons through magnetic coils at the sample. The TEM recorded how much the electrons penetrated the sample, creating a detailed picture called a micrograph. June was so skilled at preparing samples and using the TEM, her sharp micrograph images appeared in many scientific publications and textbooks.

June working with an electron microscope

JUNE ALMEIDA TIMELINE

1930

June Hart is born in Glasgow, Scotland, on October 5

1940

Brother, Harry, contracts diphtheria and dies

1942 - 1947

Attends Whitehill Senior Secondary School in Glasgow

1947

Wins Whitehill School's science prize

1947

Leaves school at age 16 to work as a laboratory technician at Glasgow Royal Infirmary

1952

Passes test to obtain an Associate of the Institute of Medical Laboratory Technology (AIMLT)

1952 - 1954

Research assistant in pathology department at St. Bartholomew's Hospital in London, England

1954

Marries Henry (Enrique) Almeida

1956 - 1964

Research assistant at the Ontario Cancer Institute in Canada, where she hones her skills with the electron microscope and negative staining technique

1960

Gives birth to daughter, Joyce

1964 - 1967

Scientific assistant at St Thomas's Hospital Medical School in London

1964

Discovers and creates an image of the first human coronavirus

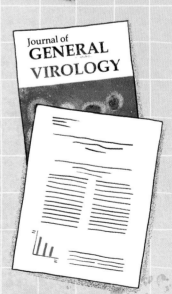

Journal of GENERAL VIROLOGY

1967

June and David Tyrrell's paper about the human coronavirus is published in the Journal of General Virology

1967

Creates first image of rubella virus

1968

Marriage to Henry ends

1967 - 1972

Research fellow and senior lecturer in the virology department at the Royal Postgraduate Medical School in London

1970

Receives master's degree from the University of London

1971

Discovers hepatitis B virus has two components

1971

Receives doctor of science from the University of London

1972

Joins Wellcome Research Laboratories in London and works on virus imaging patents and hepatitis B virus

1982

Marries virologist Phillip Samuel Gardner

1984

Retires from the field of virology

LATE 1980S

Advisor at St Thomas's Hospital Medical School and helps publish images of the HIV virus, which causes AIDS

2007

Passes away at the age of 77

SELECTED BIBLIOGRAPHY (*QUOTES FROM SOURCES WITH AN ASTERISK)

Documents supplied by Joyce Almeida: "June D. Almeida Curriculum Vitae," "June Almeida's life story," "Words and phrases to describe my mother, June Almeida."

Almeida, Joyce. "June Almeida (née Hart)." British Medical Journal 336 (June 28, 2008), https://www.ncbi.nlm.nih.gov/pmc/articles/PMC2440895/.

Almeida, June D., and Allan F. Howatson. "A Method for the Study of Cultured Cells by Thin Sectioning and Electron Microscopy." The Journal of Biophysical and Biochemical Cytology, Volume 4, Issue 1 (January 25, 1958).

Almeida, June D., and A. J. Tyrrell. "The Morphology of Three Previously Uncharacterized Human Respiratory Viruses that Grow in Organ Culture." Journal of General Virology (April 1, 1967).

*Almeida, June D. "A Classification of Virus Particles Based on Morphology." Canadian Medical Association Journal 89, no. 16 (Oct. 19, 1963).

Almeida, June D. "Practical Aspects of Diagnostic Electron Microscopy." The Yale Journal of Biology and Medicine 53 (1980): 5–18.

Combs, Sydney. "She Discovered Coronaviruses Decades Ago—But Got Little Recognition." National Geographic, April 17, 2020, https://www.nationalgeographic.com/history/2020/04/june-almeida-discovered-coronaviruses-decades-ago-little-recognition/.

Gellene, Denise. "Overlooked No More: June Almeida, Scientist Who Identified the First Coronavirus." New York Times, May 8, 2020, https://www.nytimes.com/2020/05/08/obituaries/june-almeida-overlooked-coronavirus.html.

*"June Almeida, Tribute to Scotland's Forgotten Hero of the Coronavirus," The Herald, March 7, 2020, https://www.heraldscotland.com/news/18289806.june-almeida-tribute-scotlands-forgotten-hero-coronavirus/.

Marks, Dr. Lara. "June Almeida." What Is Biotechnology, May 15, 2020, https://www.whatisbiotechnology.org/index.php/people/summary/Almeida.

Tyrrell, David and Michael Fielder. Cold Wars: The Fight Against the Common Cold. New York: Oxford University Press, 2002, 95–96.

Wu, Katherine J. "There Are More Viruses Than Stars in the Universe. Why Do Only Some Infect Us?" National Geographic, April 15, 2020, https://www.nationalgeographic.com/science/2020/04/factors-allow-viruses-infect-humans-coronavirus/

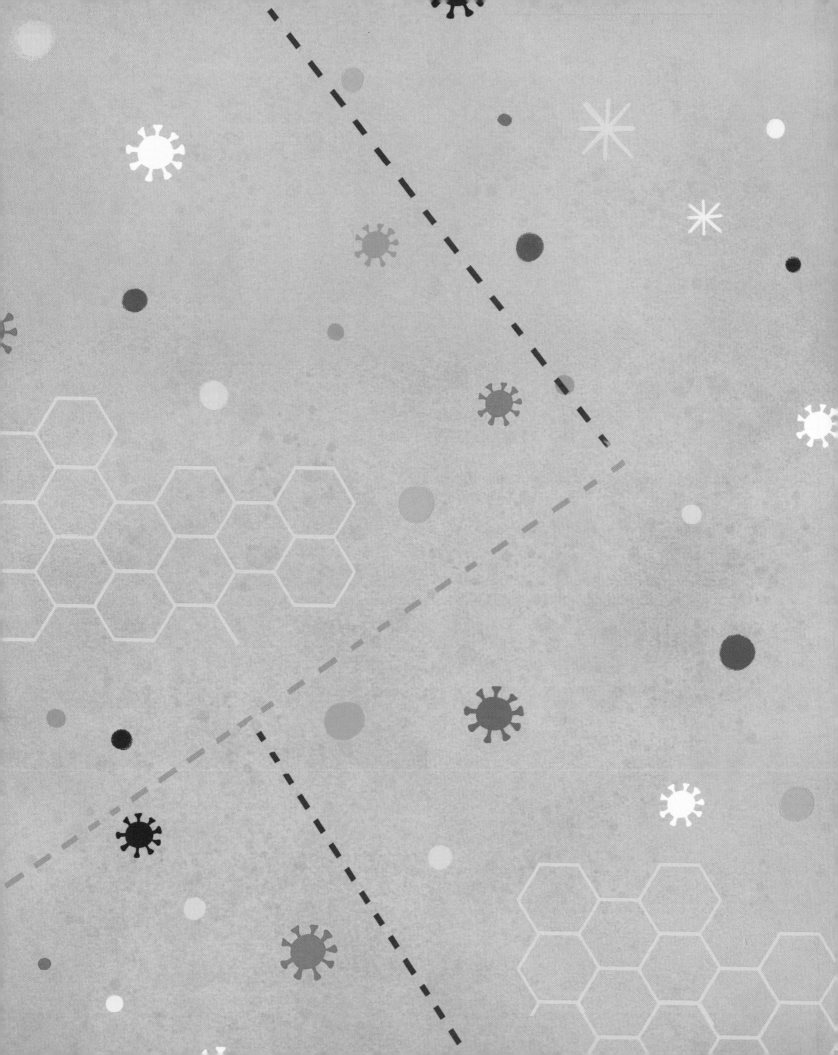